REGIS COLLEGE LIBRARY
WEST 50th & LOWELL BLVD
DENVER 11, COLORADO

D1092564

REGIS COLLEGE LIBRARY
WEST 50th & LOWELL BLVD
DENVER 11, COLORADO

SHAKSPERE'S *LOVE'S LABOR'S WON*

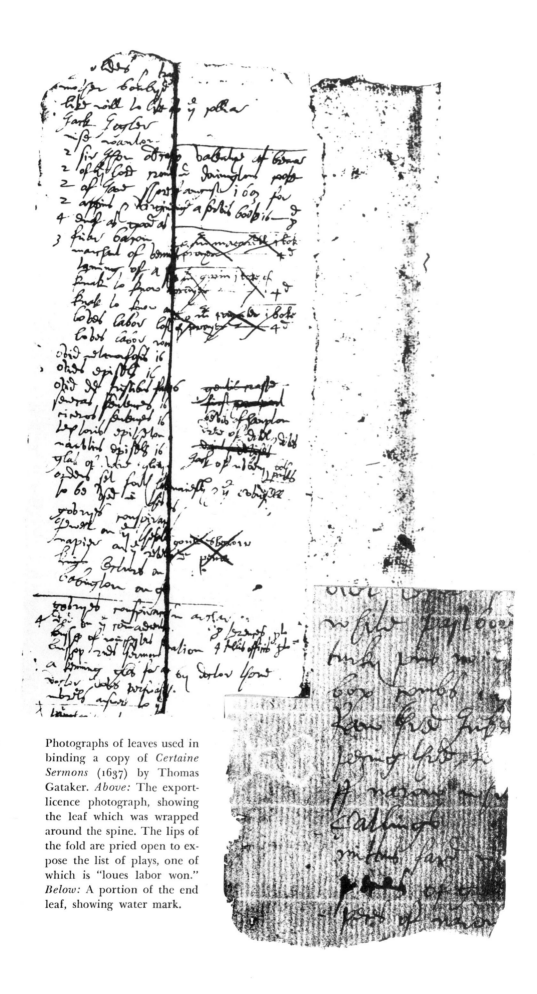

Photographs of leaves used in binding a copy of *Certaine Sermons* (1637) by Thomas Gataker. *Above:* The export-licence photograph, showing the leaf which was wrapped around the spine. The lips of the fold are pried open to expose the list of plays, one of which is "loues labor won." *Below:* A portion of the end leaf, showing water mark.

OVERSIZE
PR
2840
.B9

REGIS COLLEGE LIBRARY
WEST 50th & LOWELL BLVD
DENVER 11, COLORADO

SHAKSPERE'S
Love's Labor's Won

NEW EVIDENCE from
the *ACCOUNT BOOKS* of an
ELIZABETHAN BOOKSELLER

By

T. W. Baldwin

SOUTHERN ILLINOIS UNIVERSITY PRESS
CARBONDALE, 1957

© *1957 by*
SOUTHERN ILLINOIS UNIVERSITY PRESS
Library of Congress Catalog Card Number: 56-9515

65198

PRINTED IN THE UNITED STATES OF AMERICA
BY THE WILLIAM BYRD PRESS, INC., RICHMOND, VA.

TO
MY WIFE

PREFACE

AT THE END of the working day of the last day of 1953, as I was about to leave the Cloak Room of the British Museum, I met an obviously excited bookdealer, S. Pottesman, Esq., of whom I had been aware for many years in his preferred capacity of reader-student. We sat down on one of the backless benches of little ease to examine his find, a strip of manuscript, showing at the back hinge of a folio volume of sermons. In his magpie hobby-habit of collecting any bit of early print or manuscript, he had come upon this strip, and had noticed that it evidently contained a list of plays in 1603, some of which were Shakspere's. And there in unmistakable clarity was "loves labor won." I explained the significance of those three words and directed his agonized research for the next two or three weeks as he strove to convince himself of the obvious, that the bit of manuscript was genuine and that he, even he, had come upon an important bit of information about Shakspere.

I had communicated at once with our library, and had received orders from its Director, Dr. Robert B. Downs, to go into action. The result was that Mr. Ernest Ingold purchased the volume as yet another important contribution by him to the Shakspere material in the University of Illinois Library. Miss Helen M. Welch, Acquisition Librarian, took the volume personally to R. R. Donnelley & Sons of Chicago, who removed from the binding and straightened this and a companion piece of manuscript. The present reproduction attempts to share the material of the manuscript with all who may be interested.

At the time of discovery, I was a Fulbright Research Scholar in the

United Kingdom, affiliated with Bedford College, University of London, spending my days in the happy hunting ground of the British Museum, where the fundamental research for this volume was done.

I am particularly grateful to Dr. Sina Spiker of Southern Illinois University Press, a former pupil, for saving me a great deal of labor in getting this volume into print.

T. W. Baldwin

Urbana, Illinois
March, 1956

CONTENTS

1

THE MANUSCRIPT: ITS ORIGIN, HISTORY, AND SIGNIFICANCE

Page   3

2

THE TRANSCRIPTION

Page   17

First Leaf *Recto*

Page   21

First Leaf *Verso*

Page   31

Second Leaf *Recto*

Page   41

SHAKSPERE'S *LOVE'S LABOR'S WON*

THE MANUSCRIPT:

ITS ORIGIN, HISTORY,

AND SIGNIFICANCE

Dᴵᴰ WILLIAM SHAKSPERE write a play of *Love's Labor's Won,* as Francis Meres in 1598 said that he had? A recently discovered leaf of manuscript shows that in 1603 there was a play in print under that title, and, by associating it with *Love's Labor's Lost,* gives some support to the attribution to Shakspere by Meres.

The present volume reproduces this and another leaf of manuscript, each approximately 11 x 6¼ inches over all, taken from a copy of *Certaine Sermons* by Thomas Gataker, printed by John Haviland for Fulke Clifton, 1637, together with *Saint Stevens Last Will and Testament,* E. P. for Nicolas Bourne, 1638, which is frequently attached to it. The leaf which was at the back hinge of the volume contains a stationer's jottings in August, 1603, while the leaf which was at the front hinge contains similar jottings made about September, 1607.

1

Fᴏʀ ʜɪs end-leaves at the back of this copy of *Certaine Sermons* the binder folded a sheet of paper with a different watermark to form two folio leaves. Next, to protect the final leaves from chafing by the binding he folded the manuscript leaf of 1603 lengthwise, and then wrapped it lengthwise around the spine of these two end-leaves, with the two open edges of the folds and most of the material next to the binding, using only enough of the butt on the side next the book to catch firmly. Thus the manuscript leaf was inserted around the spine of the two end-leaves as a guard against chafing at the hinge, a usual precaution of the time.

[3]

The second end-leaf may then have been pasted to the inside of the back cover. In that case, only the doubled butt-edge of the manuscript leaf would have been visible as a stub between the book proper and the first end-leaf.

But if the second end-leaf was ever pasted to the cover it soon became detached. For there is quite a bit of ancient "doodling" on its verso, and at least one matching "doodle" appears on the manuscript of 1603, both open folds of which "lay to" the end-leaf instead of the cover, and in that way preserved the inner margin of that end-leaf from staining and "doodling," but itself acquired stain and at least one associational "doodle" in a blank space on the verso of its second fold. Thus the wrong end of the writing on the verso of this second fold has been exposed from early times, if not originally. But the front end of the list of plays, which contains the reference to "loves labor won," was on the verso of the first fold, only a few tail-end words of long titles appearing on the recto of the second fold, the center of the play list being on the section of the manuscript leaf which was wrapped around the spine of the two end-leaves. So the list would not be even partially visible unless one pried open the lips of the two folds, as Mr. Pottesman did—this particular world proving to be his oyster![1]

The manuscript leaf of 1607 was used for a guard at the front hinge, evidently around front end-leaves; but these end-leaves got pulled out of its folds—probably as good blank paper to serve some other purpose— so that they have not survived with the volume.

Three recent penciled and pasted labels are inside the front cover.

1   only four in S.T.C.

                                S.T.C.

                        11652 A. 3 √R J copy

The R and the check mark are in ink.

2   Jaggard's Copy

3 Contains famous sermon on England's delivery from Spanish Armada

There is also the penciled annotation on the inside cover itself, "Separate piece dated 1638 at end." On the turned-over leather near the top at the left are two modern initials in pencil, which I take to be M. H.

---

[1] These lips are shown open in the export-licence photograph, with an inserted pencil mark opposite the "love" plays for identification.

Since it would have no bearing on the question of the pieces of manuscript, I have made no attempt to trace the recent provenance of the volume.

The two manuscript leaves were removed and straightened by R. R. Donnelley & Sons Company of Chicago. Mr. Harold W. Tribolet of that firm wrote to Miss Welch under date of May 12, 1954: "As I told you when you visited us, our examination of the construction in the book 'Certaine Sermons' indicated that the two fragment manuscript leaves had been made part of the book during the original construction and that we are confident they were not added at a later date." In reporting to me on May 11, 1954, upon this visit Miss Welch wrote: "They not only saved all of the sewing thread but marked it in such a way that you can identify the place where each thread was removed. They also stated that the manuscript leaves were sewed in at the time the book was bound and could not have been supplied later. This fact was proved to their satisfaction by the tightness of the thread and by some small red brush marks where the ink which was used to color the edges of the book got on to the inside leaves." Thus the manuscript leaves belong to the original construction and that construction occurred shortly after the book was printed in 1637/8, as any competent judge of bindings will recognize at a glance.

I do not know whether Fulke Clifton, for whom this copy of *Certaine Sermons* was printed, did his own binding. The binder may have used other leaves from these accounts for other copies of this book or for other books bound about this time, so that other leaves may exist, if they have not already been destroyed with the old bindings. That these two leaves should have survived and should finally have been recognized for what they are is little short of miraculous. Even more remarkable is the fact that really important leaves, perhaps *the* really important leaves of the lot, are the ones which have survived.

So far as I can tell, the leaves may not have belonged originally to the same book of accounts, though both have belonged to foldings in the same format. The leaf of 1603 (the play-list leaf) has no watermark, and the chain lines run across, indicating a quarto folding. The leaf of 1607 has the chain lines across also, with the right end of a watermark, a "pot," showing in the lower left margin. It was thus also in a quarto folding. But the two leaves were not conjugate, since the left half of the watermark would in that case have shown in the lower right margin of the leaf of 1603. The binder probably reached for the most convenient waste leaf and the luck fell on these. At least, they both probably belonged to the same pile of waste if not originally to the same volume.

2

THE LEAF which was at the back hinge has on its recto numerous jottings of items sold from August 9, 1603, through August 17, 1603. All except one of these have been crossed off, though in one case the remaining sum of 3s. was to be transferred "into my debt booke." This notation is in a different hand, which was probably also responsible for a few corrections. With this exception, all entries upon this page appear to be in the same hand, which is the same as the principal hand on the verso. The reference to "my debt booke" would seem to imply that this correction and notation is in the hand of the owner of the shop. Out of order at the foot of the page was a bill of schoolbooks for a schoolmaster on August 13, 1603. Immediately above this list are three jottings, with purpose and date unspecified. The blank space between these items and the entries on the upper half of the page has caught one "doodle," when the verso of the second end-leaf received its extraornamentation. It is clear, therefore, that here on the recto of this manuscript leaf are day-book jottings of some stationer's shop for August 9 through August 17, 1603.

On the verso, the only date is in a similar notation for August 19, 1603, which was inserted after the main list of books was made. This main list, therefore, was made before August 19, 1603, presumably though not certainly after August 17 and close to August 19, since the ink and the handwriting of the entry of August 19 match that of the main list. With a quill pen and variable ink that fact is important, especially if one wrote rather heavily as this man did. First came a list of sixteen plays (lines 2–17) under the heading "[inter]ludes & tragedyes" (line 1). Since one of these plays was *Cromwell* (line 7), entered S.R. August 11, 1602, this list of plays is certainly appreciably later than that date, and, as we have seen, certainly earlier than August 19, 1603. Then follow seven schoolbooks, without separate heading, but at a slightly different angle on the paper, indicating clearly a shift in position on the part of the penman, and consequently some interval of elapsed time. At least some of these books were probably printed in 1603.[2] There are

---

[2] See notes to lines 18–24.

then seven other items (lines 25–32), mostly sermons, probably jotted down at another "sitting." Of these items, all except one had been printed in more than one edition, and there is nothing to limit our dates. The exception is the "orders set forth lately" for the plague (lines 26–27). Dr. F. S. Ferguson has, independently of my identical conclusion, identified this for me as *S.T.C.* 9209, July 30, 1603. Since we must allow a few days for print and distribution, our list could have dated only a few days before August 19. Items on the recto are dated August 9, Tuesday; August 10, Wednesday; August 12, Friday; and August 17, Wednesday. Our one date on the verso is the following Friday, August 19. For the list on this verso, the leaf might readily have been turned at any time after the recto began to be occupied on Tuesday, August 9; but the state of the pen and the consequent inking match best with the entry of Friday, August 19.

Below this main list on the verso a line has been drawn, and seven items—he seems to have believed in sevens!—mostly sermons, have been listed. But the first item is Gowry's *Conspiracy* (line 33), "yᵉ last," which would be the edition of 1603. For Dod on the commandments (line 34), *S.T.C.* gives an entry of September 6, 1603, but I have not found the entry, nor any entry for September, 1603. Bilson's sermon (line 35) was entered August 9, by Clement Knight, and in the nature of the case would have been available shortly after. Rudd's sermon (line 36) was entered June 27, 1603 by Man and Clement Knight, and being topical would also have been available shortly after. Thorne's *Kenning-glasse* (line 37) was entered June 15, 1603. Dove's *Persuasion* (line 38) had been printed in 1602 and reprinted 1603. Muriell's *Answer* (line 39), which, incidentally, was not "Anon." to this bookseller even though the book does not name the author, was entered June 25, 1603. Thus, these are items printed June to August, 1603, unless Dod does belong to September 6.

There was finally a separate item at the bottom of the page (line 40) which I cannot decipher. The left-over right margin has been used for jottings of account, the first of which is dated August 19, 1603. The other jottings are undated but must be about the same period.

As to the scribe, most of the writing is in the same hand as the recto. But four of the jottings in the right margin (lines 11b–16b, 29b–30b) are in a different hand, which does not appear on the recto.

The other leaf, that of 1607, has writing only on the recto, appar-

[7]

ently in one hand only. This hand does not appear to be the same as any hand occurring on the leaf of 1603.

Since these are not particularly distinctive hands, I have made no attempt to identify them. For even if we should be able to identify the shop from which they came, we still would not know the personnel and their various handwritings well enough to draw any trustworthy conclusions. At least, I do not regard myself as being sufficiently expert to draw any conclusions that I would trust.

3

Most of the entries in these leaves are concerned with books; but in 1603 one item was "string'd wth ribon," there were "gilt piners," fancy writing tables, a small loan, book-binding, "1 farest 8 d pener." The leaf of 1607 shows the nonbook side of the business. Besides the "absyes," primers, and testaments for petty school, there is a large inventory of playing cards, shoehorns, inkle of numerous varieties, together with filleting, for the ornamentation of various wares, such as inkhorns and penners. There were sand boxes, pins in various shapes and colors, thread, laces, points, paste boards, combs, catlings, mittens faced with colored fur, yellow latten, brass counters, hog rings, hour glasses, slickstones, latten bells, hand flaskets, brushes, braided silk, "girdels of sondry sortes," tinsel and lace, looking glasses, links, yellow wax candles. Many of these items, such as inkhorns and penners, would naturally be carried by a stationer, and many of the other items were for the ornamentation of these and similar wares. The looking glass, for instance, reminds us of the fancy "book" described by Shakspere in Sonnet LXXVII. And if this stationer lists no dials, he did at least have hourglasses. But these items of ornamentation evidently "attracted" others of similar nature—like girdles and hog rings!—so that this stationer ran a kind of "five and ten" or Woolworth's. Here is an amusing and even enlightening glimpse into actuality. When Shakspere entered a stationer's shop, we know some of the "notions" he would likely have found there to coax the pennies out of his pockets.

This stationer dealt heavily in schoolbooks. It is quite satisfactory to find him supplying a group of such books for "m^r elmes scholm^r of gillingam" in Dorset, including Camden's Greek grammar, along with other works for the highest reaches of grammar school. There is also a grammar, doubtless Lily, supplied for Giles Batter of Winterbourne, in

Dorset. A penny absey hornbook to Henry Axford shows care for the needs of the petty school, which in 1607 was to be fully supplied with A-B-C's with catechism, primers, and testaments[3] through Edward Dight at Exeter. Seven grammar-school texts appear grouped in one list of 1603. Sold or for sale were eight copies of Terence and four of Cicero's *De Officiis*. It is clear that one could get any of the usual texts for petty school or grammar school from this dealer.[4]

As prominent as schoolbooks were the numerous religious books. A dozen or so of these appear, along with the Book of Common Prayer, mostly of current materials. There were four copies of Dod on the commandments, while Bishop Rudd's sermon before the King at Greenwich was in demand. Similar sermons by Bilson and Blague also appear. Besides these, however, there was such solid diet as Perkins, Jewel on Thessalonians, Napier on Revelation, King on Jonas, Babington on Genesis, etc. If one wished books for edification, they were in excellent supply at this shop.

One could, however, find quite a bit of *belles lettres* of a sort. Mr. Hawkins' brother-in-law had a copy of Tasso's *Godfrey of Bulloigne* in Fairfax's translation, along with *Gesta Romanorum* and *Seven Wise Masters*, the last in probably an elderly edition. Similar but somewhat lighter fare was available in Deloney's *Gentle Craft*, in *Bevis of Hampton*, Edward's *Dainty Devices*, and Deloney's *Jack of Newbury*, but not in Lupton's *Devil and Dives*. No one was likely to be seriously corrupted by such as these.

But we are likely to fall most avidly upon the least characteristic offering, the sixteen plays—what a fortune did this bookseller have in his hands! A good proportion of them were quite elderly and no doubt had been accumulated somewhere in stock—his or someone else's. He would probably have jumped at the chance of getting a sixpence for one of these, such as the four copies of Wager's *Enough is as good as a Feast*, of

[3] I have a copy of the Erasmus *Paraphrase* which evidently served the New Testament function in some group of petties in north Dorset, as is witnessed by the scribbles of numerous boys in its margins and blank spaces. One writes, "This is Richard Strangwaye his bouck Record of henry Clark of Marnhull." I am sorry to report that an anonymous admirer felt impelled to record that "Ric. Strang-

waies is a rascall roge & a lobcocke asse." "Robard Pope of marnhull in the county of Dorset" and numerous others also try their pens and their inventions. One faint scrawl looks to be "Luforus schole."

[4] For the uses of these texts, see T. W. Baldwin, *William Shakspere's Petty School*, and *William Shakspere's Small Latine and Lesse Greeke*.

around 1565, not to mention other ancients. He did not go in for the latest plays as he did the latest sermons—you could turn your money rapidly on sermons. The fact that someone was willing to risk three fairly recent plays by Shakspere is quite a compliment—or is it? Altogether, this dealer offered very substantial fare. His customers had to be religious, patriotic, antipapal, "the salt of the earth"! Neither Papists nor Puritans would find any crumb of comfort here. If we may judge by his stock, he could have described himself in the words of Edward Fairfax, translator of his *Godfrey of Bulloigne,* as "neither a fantastic Puritan nor superstitious Papist, but so settled in conscience that I have the sure ground of God's word to warrant all I believe, and the commendable ordinances of our English Church to approve all I practise."[5]

4

WE INQUIRE, therefore, for whom this bookdealer catered. The geographical connections are quite pronounced. On August 13, for instance, "m^r Coles at sir e[d]mond ludlowes" of Hill Deveril, Hundred of Heytesbury, in Wiltshire left two shillings to pay for part of Perkins' *Work.* The same day, Richard, Sir William Dorington's cater at Breamore in Hampshire had three items concerned with the new King: (1) the "naration" of his coming, and (2) and (3) sermons by Doctors Rudd and Blague before the King. Richard shows the same interest in the coronation of 1603 as did very numerous Englishmen in that of 1953. Also on the same day Jerome Morris of Gillingham in Dorset had procured for Mr. Elmes, the schoolmaster, not only four characteristic schoolbooks for his "Greeks," but also an *Anatomy of Popish Tyranny* to enable him to care for the health of their souls, as well as Barrough's *Method of Physic,* and Sir Thomas Elyot's *Castle of Health* for the health of their bodies. And, of course, writing tables, perhaps among other things to set down a reckoning of their sins against them. The reading of this small section of Wilts-Hants-Dorset was quite sound educationally, religiously, and politically. No copy of *Love's Labor's Won* is likely to have strayed into their area through these worthies.

But the connections with the area are not confined to the one day of August 13. Already on the first day of our record, August 9, Thomas Webb's wife of Winterbourne, Dorset, had bought one grammar, evidently Lily, for Giles Batter of Winterbourne. Learning was to flourish

---

[5] *DNB, s.v.* Fairfax, Edward.

at Winterbourne in southern Dorset as it was at Gillingham in the north. Gillingham grammar school is known to Carlisle but not Winterbourne. Had it a grammar school also or did the petty master act the part of Holofernes? On the last day of our record, as on the first, the region is represented. On August 19, Valentine, who was Sir William Dorington's cook at Breamore, had a service book bound. In fact, all our definite references to locality in this eleven-day period belong to this same area. One wishes that some local antiquary would tell us more about Mr. Coles, Richard the cook, Valentine the caterer, Mr. Elmes the schoolmaster, and the Webbs and Batter at Winterbourne.[6]

Why do these localizations of 1603 all belong to the one area, Dorset-Hampshire-Wiltshire? An at first ambiguous entry on the leaf for 1607 gives the clue. It commands, "direct a letter to edward dighte to be delivered at christofer hvnts in pater noster rew nere ye Kings hed in london september 1607"[7] three petty school books in quantity. Now Edward Dight was a bookseller and bookbinder of Exeter,[8] evidently succeeding Christopher Hunt there. He was probably the nephew Edward Dight, to whom Walter Dight, printer in London from 1590, left his "quiar bookes" in 1618. This Walter was the son of John Dight of Dunyate, co. Somerset.[9] So Edward Dight was no doubt also from Somerset, and thus local to the region.

Christopher Hunt's record will explain the rest. On January 12, 1585, "**Christofer Hunt** son of **Walter Hunt** of **Blan[d]ford** in ye county of **Dorset** Cordwa[i]ner . . . put him selfe Apprentice to **Thomas man** citizen and Staconer of London for terme of Eight yeres from ye feast of ye Birth of our lord [25 December] 1584."[10] So on October 2, 1592, he was "sworne and admytted A freman of this Companie."[11] He made as his first entry, January 26, 1594, "a booke called **Godfrey** of *Bolloigne* an heroyalcall poem of Sir **Torquato Tasso** Englisshed. / . by R E Esquier."[12] This translation of part of *Godfrey* by R. Carew was printed in 1594 by J. Windet for "*C. Hunt of Exceter,*" showing that Hunt had already located at Exeter. There is also an undated issue by Windet for Man,

---

[6] It is a great relief, however, that there is no mention of Cerne Abbas, and no copy of *Willobie his Avisa* for sale!

[7] One should remember the "impersonal style" of Elizabethan advertising: "In such great letters as they write 'Here is good horse to hire'." (*Much Ado,* I, i, 267–68).

[8] R. B. McKerrow, *A Dictionary of Printers and Booksellers,* p. 92.

[9] *Ibid.,* p. 93.

[10] Arber, II, 130.

[11] Arber, II, 711.

[12] Arber, II, 644.

the former master of Hunt. The later verse translation by E. Fairfax, printed 1600, for Jaggard and Lownes appears in our manuscript of 1603. A few days later than the entry of *Godfrey*, on February 1, 1594, Hunt was fined £3 "for buyinge and dispersinge of *psalmes* Disorderly printed."[13] The sum would indicate that Christopher had indulged heavily.

On May 5, 1606, Hunt entered "A ballett called *the shamefull Downefall of the popes Kingdome conteynninge the lyfe and deathe of* Stephen Garnett *the popes Cheife preiste in England* &c."[14] On May 26, 1606, he brought to book a local celebrity of southwest England in "a booke called *the Paricide papiste / or Cutt throate Catholique beinge A Tragicall Discourse of a murther latelie committed at Padstowe in the countie of Cornewall by a professed papiste Killinge his owne father and afterwards himself in Zeale of his popishe religion.*"[15] Quite clearly, Hunt had no leanings to the papists. Under King James, Hunt had also a patent to "print a booke in Englishe called the *Householders practise.*"[16]

So Christopher Hunt of Blandford in Dorset had set up business in Exeter, where in 1603 he was supplying books to his old neighbors;[17] but before September, 1607, he had returned to London and located in Paternoster Row, near where he had been an apprentice under Thomas Man, who was at the Talbot in Paternoster Row.[18] The location is itself significant. For Paternoster Row "was probably named from the makers of paternosters, or beads, who lived there; later it was occupied by stationers and textwriters, who sold copies of the Paternoster, Ave, Creed, etc. In the 16th cent. it was taken possession of by the mercers, and was the fashionable shopping st. for the ladies."[19] Hunt's stock in 1607 reflects exactly its locale. Now we understand the reason for those frippery items!

But by 1638, Hunt's old day books were no longer of use in their original function and so their leaves were translated among other things into guards for bindings, two leaves serving to protect a copy of Gataker's

---

[13] Arber, II, 821.

[14] Arber, III, 320.

[15] Arber, III, 322.

[16] Arber, V, lvii.

[17] With the plague raging in London, the booktrade there in August, 1603, was practically nonexistent—"Lord have mercy upon us!" If one may judge by entries S. R., June had flourished, July dwindled. Then after August 1, there was one entry S. R. August 8, four August 9, three August 15, none in September, nor in the first two weeks of October. Certainly our record of sales in August, 1603, is not for London.

[18] McKerrow, *Dictionary*, p. 184.

[19] E. H. Sugden, *A Topographical Dictionary*, p. 394.

Certaine Sermons—a supremely fitting end for them. That these fragments have now come to rest in "the Bible Belt" along with a complete collection of Milton firsts and similar monuments of "insularity and provincialism" is, I hope, no less fitting.

If this is a correct account of the place of origin for the lists of 1603, then their reason for being is also reasonably clear. These would be books newly received from London, doubtless by "carrier," whose schedule would throw light on the probable time of arrival. Many of these books were recently printed. The plague pamphlet, for instance, must have started for Exeter hot off the press, since it was entered S.R. July 30. Such an annotation in the second list as that one of the books was "for m^r archar" points also to a local agent, buying on order. If these books were new arrivals from London, then Hunt had recently bought out someone's accumulated stock of plays in London—accumulated as shown by the considerable number of old-timers in it. As to whose stock, I see no way for that disturbed period of making even a profitable guess.[20]

5

THE CHIEF interest of the manuscript for most of us, I suppose, is its proof that a play called "loves labor won" was in August, 1603, to be had in print. Our only other mention of the play in early days occurs in a list of Shakspere's plays by Francis Meres in 1598. "For Comedy, witnes his *Gētlemē of Verona*, his *Errors*, his *Loue labors lost*, his *Loue labours wonne*, his *Midsummers night dreame*, & his *Merchant of Venice*."[21] Since Meres balances six comedies against six tragedies, and since no play survives under the title of *Love's Labor's Won*, some have suspected that Meres manufactured the title in antithesis to *Love's Labor's Lost* in order to have six comedies to balance against six tragedies. Meres is now cleared from that suspicion; there was a play printed under the title of *Love's Labor's Won*. While it is now clear that by 1598 there were six comedies and six tragedies attributable to Shakspere, it by no means follows that Shakspere had at that date written only

[20] The stock had been active, however, well after August 11, 1602, since it contained a copy of *Cromwell*, entered S.R. on that date. The occasion for disposing of this stock of plays thus arose in the last quarter of 1602 or the first half of 1603. The spread of the printers and publishers involved in the plays indicates that the stock belonged neither to a regular publisher nor to a printer, but to an ordinary stationer—the vast majority, which we tend to forget.

[21] Meres, *Palladis Tamia* (1598), fol. 282^r (Ernest Ingold copy, U. of Ill. Lib.).

six comedies and only six tragedies. An even dozen, balancing six and six was such a comfortable number; it would not do, for instance, to leave such a list at sixes and sevens! Nor do we know that Meres would have classified all of Shakspere's plays as either tragedies or comedies; those who organized the First Folio did not.[22] Simply, we are now assured that the twelve plays which Meres mentions did exist and were attributable to Shakspere.

Our new record, however, does not tell us whether *Love's Labor's Won* itself has perished or whether it has survived under a different title. Obviously, *Love's Labor's Won,* was not *Merchant of Venice* or *Love's Labor's Lost,* since they occur in the same list. Nor for similar reasons would it have been *Two Gentlemen of Verona, The Comedy of Errors,* or *Midsummer-Night's Dream,* which occur additionally in Meres' list. Since the stationer in 1603 has used the actual title or part thereof in all other cases, he has presumably done so with this play also, confirmed by the fact that Meres gives the same title. As a matter of fact, the stationer conforms to the tradition of print while Meres does not. For our scribe uses the form "loves labor lost" and "loves labor won." It is clear that this was the basic form of the title. As the title of the former play, the quarto of 1598 gives *Loues labors lost* on the title page, which is interpreted in all the running heads as *Loues Labor's lost.* In the First Folio, the *Catalogue* of plays lists it as *Loues Labour lost,* while the title and running heads follow the first quarto in using *Loues Labour's lost.* The tradition of print, therefore, is that the second word of each title is clearly singular and not plural. The tradition divides, however, as to whether *labor* should be followed by apostrophe "s" for "is." Expressed or omitted, the sense is the same, "Love's Labor is Lost." Meres is thus out of the tradition of print with his *"Loue labors lost, his Loue labours wonne."* The authoritative form is that of the first quarto, *Love's Labor's Lost,* which is the usual form of the present day. Our stationer, therefore, is in the tradition of print, as he should be.

Also, unless the play had already been reprinted under another title, as is not probable, it is not likely that it was any other of the comedies which were in print by 1603. The only others known and not previously ruled out are *Merry Wives of Windsor* and *Much Ado About Nothing.* Thus our stationer had three of the six comedies of Shakspere which

---

[22] For a usual further classification of "history," which such a pedant as Meres would surely have known, see Marvin T. Herrick, *Tragicomedy,* pp. 215 ff.

are now known to have been in print, lacking *Midsummer-Night's Dream, Merry Wives of Windsor,* and *Much Ado About Nothing.*

The First Folio classifies fourteen plays as comedy. Of these, it seems generally agreed that *The Tempest* and *The Winter's Tale* are considerably later than 1603 in any form. *As You Like It,* along with *Much Ado,* was "staied" August 4, 1600; so it is not a likely candidate. The majority would probably agree that *Twelfth Night* is later than the mention of *Love's Labor's Won* by Meres in 1598, thus eliminating it as a probability. The *Taming of the Shrew* must have had at least a *Shrew* in its title from the outset, since the word is indigenous to the background as it is to the two surviving titles and to contemporary references. The theme was proverbial and the play titles inevitable; they were shrew plays, not love plays. We have left, therefore, as suspicious characters *Measure for Measure,* and *All's Well that Ends Well.* In character pattern, etc., *All's Well* is closest of all the plays to *Love's Labor's Lost,* so that I have long considered it to be the most likely candidate.[23] But this mention in 1603, while it eliminates some plays entirely and others probably, yet it does not indicate directly whether *Love's Labor's Won* survives at all, nor if so under what title. Consequently, there would be no point to reviewing here all the suggested identifications of *Love's Labor's Won* with various plays of Shakspere. Simply, we are now assured that in August, 1603, there was in print a play called *Love's Labor's Won,* which Meres attributes directly to Shakspere, as does our stationer by indirection.

[23] See *Organization and Personnel* and succeeding works. It appears certain that the present form of *All's Well* represents a revision later than our mentions of *Love's Labor's Won* in 1598 and 1603. If *All's Well* should be a revision of the earlier play, then the change of title would readily have been occasioned by the revision. If a copy of *Love's Labor's Won* is ever discovered, it is not likely to be exactly the folio version of *All's Well.*

THE TRANSCRIPTION

I HAVE TRIED to arrange the transcription so that with the aid of an occasional note the ordinary scholar can follow my interpretation of the essential facts in the facsimile. Since the experts will not need a transcription, I have made no attempt to represent finical details of paleography. I have numbered each line of each page and have arranged my notes accordingly. When a line is divided in content, I have referred to the inserted matter to the right of the page as *b*. I have identified the English books by their numbers in the *Short Title Catalogue* and have quoted the descriptions of the various editions available by August, 1603. Upon occasion I have supplemented this information. For plays, I have added the number in Sir Walter Greg's *Bibliography*, to which the reader is advised to turn for fuller information. I have thought it best to put as much of the technical, reference information as possible into the notes so as not unduly to clutter my introduction. The reader can thus check my conclusions by the facts if he wishes.

I have not discussed prices of books, since they are few and would require to be interpreted in a much larger framework than can be given them here. It is interesting to know that at least one penny-hornbook actually did sell for a penny (Leaf 1_r, line 7). Some of the gross prices (Leaf 2_r, lines 4–6) particularly will need interpretation. But such questions of price could be treated adequately only in a separate study.

First Leaf *Recto*

[1603, BACK HINGE]

To thomas wolf ? de of ?rimtrimund the 9th
august 1603 for ? batt. of ?rimtr ?
i grammer   paid   i   o

        to henry Oxford ? y e of august   i   6   9
        i day ly ? of a christia string
        ? bar. it ? i ? ? i ? alle

in ? at fiu ? 1603 ludlowes left to pay
for part of ? work on ? ? day of august

        to richard ? ? ? ? ? y 13 of august
i narration of ? 1603 ? out of holland   4
i dotar ? ? sermon   bj
i dotar blague ? sermon

        To ? ? ? brother law y 17 august 1603
i ? of ? i folio ———————————————— 5   0
i gesta romanor ———————————————— 0   8
i ? ? ? ? ———————————————————— 0   6
6 ? ? ? ? in part of payment 3   ?
    ? 6 0 ? ? ? into my ? booke

dotar ? ? sermon   lent ? ? by ?
dotar blague ? ? on   ? ? ? y 17 august
gill pinder   1603
                              in money pay 3
i ? ? to ?
i ? ? ? ? ? ?
? of ?
? of ?
12 ? ? ? ?
i ? ? ?   To ? morris for
i ? ?   ? ? ? of ?
? ?   y 13 of august 1603

1 To thomas webs wife of winterburne the 9th [of]

2 august 1603 for Giles batter of winterburne

3 1 graīer ——————————————— 1^s — 0

4 ————————— paid

5 to henry Axford ye x of august ———

6 1 dayly exe[rc]ise of a christiā stringd —1^s—3^d

7 wth ribon —14^d & 1 horne absye 1^d alle

8 1603

9 m^r Coles at sir e[d]mond ludlowes left to paye

10 for part of perkins work on ye 13 day of august 2^s

11 william

12 to richard sir ʌ dorringtons cater ye 13 of august

13 1603

14 1 naration of y^e [king]s coming out of scotland — 4^d

15 1 doctor rud his sermon

16 1 doctor blague his sermon ——————————vj^d

17 To yong m^r havkins brotherin law ye 17 august 1603

18 1 godfry of bull[en] in follio ——————— 5^s — 6

19 1 gesta romanorū ————————————— 0 —— 8

20 s 1 seven wise masters ———————————— 0 —— 6

21 6—8^d received in part of payment ——3^s —8^d

22 rest—3s—0 rest—[3]s—6d

23 payed into my debt booke

24 Jhon

25 doctor rud his sermon lent m^r thornbery by his

26 doctor blague his sermon boy peter ye 17 august

27 1603

28 gilt piners

29 ———————————————— in monye ——— 3^s

30 barowes method to physik payd

31 writing tables wth callenders & gold waytes

32 castell of helth

33 anotomy of popish [ti]rannie

34 2 licosthenes apoth[em]s lardg 8to

35 cambdins grek gr[a]mers To Jeram morris for

36 textors epitheto[n] 16 m^r elmes scholm^r of gillingam

37 [Tho]matias dictionarye ye 13 of august 1603

3 Probably a copy of Lily's Latin grammar of the current edition.

6 I do not know what this was.

7 A hornbook of some current issue.

9 Sir Edmond Ludlow was knighted by the queen September 14, 1601, at Basing, at the Marquis of Winchester's (Stowe, *Annales* [1605], p. 1411; Nichols, *Progresses of Elizabeth*, III, 567; Wm. A. Shaw, *Knights of England*, II, 99). He was of Hill Deverill in Wiltshire. For him and the Ludlow family, see R. C. Hoare, *The History of Modern Wiltshire; Hundred of Heytesbury*, pp. 13 ff. Mr. Coles was doubtless one of the numerous preacher-schoolmasters of the name.

10 *S.T.C.* 19647 —The works of that famous a. worthie minister of Christ in the vniuersitie of Cambridge, M. W. Perkins: gathered into one volume a. newly corrected acc. to his owne copies. 18 pts. pp. 939. fol. *J. Legate, printer to the Vniuer. of Cambridge,* 1603.

A reprint of the preceding with five additional treatises. The title to 'An Exposition of the Lords prayer' has the imprint: *Printed f. J. Porter a. R. Jackson,* 1602.
Our jotting indicates that the *Works* could be had in parts.

11 The scribe first wrote "richard m^r dorringtons cater." The suspended *r* is still in place. He or someone else later inserted *s,* dotted the first minim of the *m* to make an *i,* and tinkered the rest into an *r.* The resultant "sir" called for a proper name, which he inserted above the line, exactly, as it proved, where it would get injured when the leaf was used for binding. But enough is clear to show that the name was "william," which external circumstances confirm.

For later, on August 19, we have an entry for "valentyne at bremor was m^r doringtons cooke" (verso, line 6b). Breamore is in a tip of Hampshire between Wilts and Dorset, and there William Dorington or Dodington "About 1580 . . . acquired the Manor of Breamore in Hampshire, where he made his residence and established his family seat" (C. A. Bradford, *William Dodington: A Tragedy of St. Sepulchre's, Holborn, in 1600* [reprinted from

Transactions of the London and Middlesex Archaeological Society,
New Series, Vol. VII, Part I], p. 126). Of him we are told on April
12, 1600, that **"Dodington,** rich Dodington, yesterday morning, went
up to St. Sepulchre's Steeple, and threw himself over the battle-
ment, and broke his neck" (*ibid.,* p. 124). "He belonged to an old
Somersetshire family of which *his* branch had settled at Woodland,
in the Parish of Meare, Co. Wilts. His father was John Dodington,
an Auditor who dwelt in Bartholomew Close, London . . . . His
son, also William, was knighted by James I at his coronation in
1603" (*ibid.,* pp. 124–25). This Sir William was dubbed at White-
hall July 23, 1603 (John Philipot, *A perfect Collection or Catalogue of all Knights Batchelaurs made by King James* [1660], p, 17,
who places him in *"Dors.";* John Nichols, *Progresses . . . of King
James the First,* I, 214; Wm. A. Shaw, *Knights of England,* II, 118,
who lists him as "Dorset (Hants.)." He was thus one of the forty-
pound knights, "gregarious in a flock" along with Sir Francis
Bacon. So his fire-new stamp of honor was as yet scarce current in
August 1603, and evidently sat but rawly upon him—there must
have been a host of such mishaps! But someone later did him
proper honor by squeezing "sir william" into the first entry. One
wonders if Richard expected to find Sir William among the numerous new knights of the "naration" he had bought.

14   *S.T.C.* 14433 —A true narration of the entertainment of his
       Maiestie from his departure from Edenbrough, till his re-
       ceuing at London. *T. Creede f. T. Millington,* 1603.

15   Rudd; see verso, line 36.

16   Blague; *S.T.C.* 3121 —A sermon preached at the charterhouse
       bef. the kings maiestie, 10 May 1603. 8°. *S. Stafford,* 1603.

18   Tasso; *S.T.C.* 23698 —Godfrey of Bulloigne. Done into verse by
       E. Fairefax. [Anon.] fol. *A Hatfield f. J. Jaggard a. M. Lownes,*
       1600. Ent. 22 no. 1599.

The scribe first wrote 5^s 4^d here. The bottom of the s did not get
opened out into the usual form. The 4 was formed almost exactly
as that in line 14 above, and the connecting line for the lost d shows
at the right. Thus the three items as first set down amounted to
6^s 6^d, and this was the sum first set down in the margin at line 21.

The purchaser paid 3ˢ 8ᵈ, leaving a "rest" which was set down apparently as 3ˢ and certainly 6ᵈ, the amount being certainly wrong as to pence. At some time later, corrections were made. The 4ᵈ of line 18 was altered to 6ᵈ, and the consequent total was raised by 2ᵈ to become 6ˢ 8ᵈ, which would leave a "rest" of 3ˢ, as is now noted, with the further notation "payed into my debt booke." These two jottings are in a different hand, the latter item indicating the owner. Presumably it was he who made the corrections as well, including a strengthening of the 6 in line 20. He may also be responsible for the tinkering above at lines 11 and 12.

19 *S.T.C.* 21287 —Here after foloweth the hystorye of Gesta Romanorum. 4°. *J Kynge,* 1557.

   21288 —A record of auncient histories, Gesta Romanorum, newly perused by R. Robinson. 8°. *T. Est,* 1595.

   Numerous editions of this work do not yet appear in *S.T.C.* See Charles C. Mish, "Best Sellers in Seventeenth-Century Fiction," *Papers of the Bibliographical Society of America,* XLVII (1953), 360–61.

20 *S.T.C.* 21297 —[Seven Wise masters of Rome] 4°. [*R. Pynson,* 1493.]

   21298 —*fol.* 2. Here begynneth thystorye of yᵉ vii wyse Maysters of rome. 4°. *W. de worde,* [1520?].

   21299 —[Anr. ed.] Sig. A₂. Here beginneth thystory, etc. 8°. *W. Copland,* [*c.* 1555?] Ent. to. T. Marsh 1558–59.

23/24 In the blank space between these lines, at the exposed left edge, one "doodle" landed when the verso of the second end-sheet received its assorted varieties.

25a Rudd; see verso, line 36.

25b One John Thorneburye took up his freedom as a stationer May 17, 1614 (Arber, III, 684). The John Thornbury of our jottings, however, was likely an older man, and was, no doubt, an Exeter worthy, along with his boy Peter.

26 See 16, above.

28 Many varieties and constituents of penners appear in the list of

1607, since they were necessarily in great demand at a stationer's shop.

30 *S.T.C.* 1508 —The method of phisicke. fol. *T. Vautroullier.* 1583.
    1509 —[Anr. ed.] 4°. *R. Field,* 1590. Ent. 2 mr.
    1510 —Third ed. 4°. *R. Field,* 1596.
    1511 —[Anr. ed.] 4°. *R. Field,* 1601.

31 Evidently a fancy affair, such as Shakspere refers to in Sonnet LXXVII. Too bad he doesn't tell us the price! We might have learned how much Shakspere was "out of pocket" and so have calculated his probable profit or loss.

32 Elyot; *S.T.C.* 7643—The castel of helth. 8°. *in æd. T. Bertheleti,* 1539.
    7644 —[Anr. ed.] Corrected and augmented. ff. 94. 4° *in æd. T. Bertheleti,* 1541.
    7645 —[Anr. ed.] Corrected and augmēted. 8°. *in æd. T. Bertheleti,* 1541.
    7646 —[Anr. ed.] Corrected and augmented. 8°. *in æd. T. Bertheleti,* 1541 [or rather 1544?].
    7647 —[Anr. ed.] The castell of helth; corrected and augmented. ff. 90. 8°. *T. Berthelet,* 1541 [or rather 1548–49?].
    7648 —[Anr. ed.] The castel of helth, etc. 8°. *in æd T. Bertheleti,* 1547.
    7649 —[Anr. ed.] 8°. *in the house late T. Berthelettes* [1559?].
    7650 —[Anr. ed.] The castell of helth, etc. 8°. *T. Powell,* [1560?].
    7651 —[Anr. ed.] The castel of helth, etc. 8°. *T. Marshe,* 1561.
    7652 —[Anr. ed.] The castell of helth, etc. 8°. *T. Marshe,* 1572.
    7653 —[Anr. ed.] 8°. *T. Marshe,* 1580.
    7654 —[Anr. ed.] The castel of helth. 8°. [*London,* 1580?].
    7655 —[Anr. ed.] The castell of health. 8°. *T. Marsh,* 1587. Ent. to T. Orwin, 23 jn. 1591.
    7656 —[Anr. ed.] Corrected. 4°. *the widdow Orwin,* 1595.

33 Bell; *S.T.C.* 1814—The anatomie of popish tyrannie. 4°. *J. Harison f R. Bankworth,* 1603.

34 *S.T.C.* 17004 —Apophthegmata. 8°. *ap. T. Harperum pro Soc. Stat.,* 1635. Ent. to Harrison, Bishop a. Norton, 5 ja. 1579; to the partners in the English stock, 22 jn. 1631 [?1621?].

There may have been unrecorded editions,[1] but more likely the partners simply entered a claim, and then imported. This device was evidently used even when there were English editions.

For instance, an indenture for Henry Wall, apprenticed to Henry Conneway, citizen and stationer of London, survives at the hinges of a Clenardus Greek Grammar, Hanover, 1602, in my possession. The apprenticeship is recorded in Arber, II, 90. Since Conneway's will was proved on August 1, 1598 (McKerrow, *Dictionary*, p. 75), and the last record for Wall is May 27, 1599 (Arber, II, 235), the indenture was evidently waste from one shop or the other. It is clear, therefore, that this is a London binding, though I see nothing distinctive about it—pulling the spine to a wedge is hardly distinctive. While Clenardus was occasionally printed in England, it was also evidently upon occasion imported, unbound as provided by law.

35 *S.T.C.* 4511 —Institutio graecæ grammatices compendiaria in vsum regiæ scholæ Westmonasteriensis. [Anon.] 8°. *E. Bollifant pro S. Waterson,* 1595.

36a *S.T.C.* 20763; see verso, line 23.

36b Gillingham had a free school "and by the commission for charitable uses, 40 Eliz. it was decreed, among other things, that 20 marks yearly of the rents of the parish lands should be employed to maintain a school-master, to teach the children gratis. The election or removal of him shall be by the feoffees, with the advice and consent of the vicar" (John Hutchins, *The History and Antiquities of . . . Dorset*, III, 619; Nicholas Carlisle, *A Concise Description of the Endowed Grammar Schools* [1818], I, 372–73).

37 *S.T.C.* 24008 —Dictionarium linguæ Latinæ et Anglicanæ. 8° *Cantebrigiæ, ex off. T. Thomasii, Londini, ap. R. Boyle,* [1588?]. —Nunc denuo . . . recognitum. 8°. *Cantabrigiæ, ex off. Iohannis Legatt,* 1589. [U. of. Ill. Lib.]
  24009 —Tertio emendatum. 4°. *Cantabrigiæ, ex off. J. Legate, ap. A. Kitson, Londini,* 1592.

---

[1] A bookdealer has just catalogued (January, 1957) a Lycosthenes printed by J. Jackson in 1596.

24010 —Quarta editio. 8°. *Cantabrigiæ, ex off. J. Legatt, ap. A. Kitson, Londini,* 1594.

24011 —Quinta editio auctior. 4°. *Cantabrigiæ, ex off. J. Legati,* 1596.

24012 —Sexta editio. 8°. *Cantabrigiæ, ex off. J. Legati,* 1600.

The top of the initial capital T is visible. See lines 1, 17, 35b for this capital. Also the top of a following h. While this is a curious, cross-breed possessive of Thomasius (English spelling of the Latin sound adapted to the English possessive), yet it could hardly be anything else.

First Leaf *Verso*

[1603, BACK HINGE]

mother bombye

likd will to light quik ... dible ... to ... tollra

Jacke Iuglar

nise wanton

2 sir ... drawell

2 of ... lord norvell

2 of good ... ...

2 appius & virginia

4 ... as good as ...

3 frier bacon

marshall of ...

taming of a shrew

knak to know a knave

knak to know an honest man

loves labor lost

loves labor woon

... ...sis 16

... epistle 16

... ... fastord ... parke 16

... ... 16

... ... 16

... epistle 16

... epistle 16

... 12

... ...

to be ... call'd by ... matie ... ...

... conspiracy

... on ... ...

napier on ... ...

... ... on ...

babington on ...

... conspiracy ... last ... in arthar

4 ... on ...

bishop of ... ...

bishop and sermon

a ... ... for a christian ... by doctor ...

doctor ... perswasion ...

1 [inte]rludes & tragedyes

2 mother bombye

3 like will to like quoth yᵉ divell to yᵉ colliar

4 Jack Jugler

5 nise wanton

6 2 sir Jhon oldcastell

To valentyne at bremor

was mᵣ doringtons cooke

7 2 of yᵉ lord cromwell

8 2 of Jane shore

19 of august 1603 for

9 2 appius & Virginia

bindinge a servis booke 16—8ᵈ

10 4 enuf as good as afeaste

11 3 friar bacon

To mᵣ macarell 1 boke
of prayer 4ᵈ

12 marchant of vennis

13 taming of a shrew

T[o] mᵣ gwin 1 boke of
prayer 4ᵈ

14 knak to know a knave

15 knak to know an honest man

To mᵣ paynter 1 boke
of prayer 4ᵈ

16 lovcs labor lost

17 loves labor won

18 ovid metamorfosis 16

19 ovids epistels 16

gentil crafte

20 ovid de tristibus fastorū & ponto 16

first & 2nd part

21 senecas sentences 16

bevis of hampton

22 ciceros sentences 16

dreame of divel & dives

23 textoris epitheton 16

dainty devises

24 manvtius epistels 16

Jack of nvbery both
parts

25 glas of vaine glory in 12

26 orders set forth lately by yᵉ Kings maiesty & yᵉ covnsell

27 to be vsed in this tyme of siknes

28 govryes conspiracye

29 Jewell on yᵉ thesalonians

to mᵣ gouldesborow

30 napier on yᵉ revelation

1 farest 8 d pener

31 kings lectures on Jonas

32 babington on genesis

33 govryes conspiracye yᵉ last 1 for mᵣ archar

34 4 dod on yᵉ comandments in qᵗᵒ   8 terences 8ᵗᵒ

35 bushop of winchesters sermon at yᵉ coronation 4 tullis officis 8ᵗᵒ

36 bushop ruds sermon

37 a kenning glas for a christian ki[n]ge by doctor thorne

38 doctor doves perswasion to recusants

39 mvriels answer to yᵉ recusants petition

40

2   Lyly; *S.T.C.* 17084—Mother Bombie. [A comedy. Anon.] 4° *T.*
    Scarlet f. C. Burby, 1594. Ent. 18 jn.
       17085—[Anr. ed.] 4°. *T. Creede f. C. Burby,* 1598. Greg, 125.

3   Fulwell; *S.T.C.* 11473—An enterlude intituled Like wil to like
    quod the Deuel to the Colier. 4°. *J. Allde,* 1568. Ent. 1568–
    69 [c. Sept. 1568].
       11474—[Anr. ed.] A pleasant enterlude, etc. 4°. *Ed. Allde,* 1587.
    Greg, 50, adds an undated edition by J. Allde.

4   *S.T.C.* 14837—A new enterlued for chyldren to playe, named
    Jacke Jugeler. Neuer before imprented. 4°. *W. Copland,*
    [1563]. Ent. 1562–63 [c. Nov. 1562].
       14837a—[Anr. ed.] Newly imprented. 4°. *W. Copland,* [1565?].
    Greg, 35, adds another edition about 1570 by John Allde.

5   *S.T.C.* 25016—A preaty interlude called, Nice wanton. 4°. *J. Kyng,*
    1560. Ent. 10 jn.
       25017—[Anr. ed.] A pretie enterlude, etc. 4°. *J. Allde,* [1565?].
    Greg. 31.

6   *S.T.C.* 18795—The first part of the true and honorable historie
    of the life of Sir John Oldcastle. [By A. Munday and others.]
    4°. *V. S. [ims] f. T. Pavier,* 1600. Ent. 11 au.
    Greg, 166.

6b See recto, line 11.

7   *S.T.C.* 21532—The true chronicle historie of Thomas Lord Crom-
    well. 4°. *f. W. Jones,* 1602. Ent. to W. Cotton 11 au.
    Greg, 189, suggests that the printer was Richard Read and that we
    have to do with the bookseller William Jones, not the printer of
    the same name.

8   Heywood; *S.T.C.* 13341—The first and second partes of King
    Edward the fourth. [Anon.] 4°. *J. W[indet] f. J. Oxenbridge,*
    1599. Ent. to Oxenbridge a. Busbie 28 au.
       13342 —[Anr. ed.] 8°. *F. K[ingston] f. H. Lownes a. J. Oxen-*
    bridge, 1600. Ent. 23 fb. [from Busby to Lownes].
    Greg, 153, 154.
    It is interesting to know that the printed play was referred to as
    Jane Shore, for short. So was it this or another old play which

Chettle and Day were paid £2 to revamp for Worcester's men in
1603 (Greg, *Diary*, II, 235)? I am reminded by this shortened title
that when I was trying in 1931 to locate the plaque at the site of
the Curtain, of which not even the local policeman had heard,
everyone wanted to direct me to Nell Gwynne's house!

9   *S.T.C.* 1059 —A new tragicall comedie of Apius and Virginia. 4°.
      W. How f. R. Jhones, 1575. Ent. 1567–68. [*c.* Oct. 1567].
   Greg, 65.

10 Wager; *S.T.C.* 24933 —A comedy or enterlude intituled, Inough is
      as good as a feast. 4°. *J. Allde,* [1565?].
   Greg, 57.

11 Greene; *S.T.C.* 12267 —The honorable historie of frier Bacon
      and frier Bongay. 4°. *f. E. White,* 1594. Ent. 14 my. [White
      replacing A. Islip].
   Greg, 121, identifies Islip as the probable printer.

12 Shakspere; *S.T.C.* 22296 —The most excellent historie of the
      Merchant of Venice. 4°. *J. R*[*oberts*] *f. T. Heyes,* 1600. Ent.
      to J. Roberts 22 jy. 1598; to T. Haies by consent of J. Rob-
      erts 28 oc. 1600.
   Greg, 172.

13 *S.T.C.* 23667 —A pleasant conceited historie called The taming
      of a Shrew. 4°. *P. Short, sold by C. Burbie,* 1594. Ent. to Short
      2 my.
     23668 —[Anr. ed.] 4°. *P. S*[*hort*] *sold by C. Burbie,* 1596.
   Greg, 120.

14 *S.T.C.* 15027 —A most pleasant comedie, intituled, a knacke to
      know a knaue. 4°. *R. Jones,* 1594. Ent. 7 ja.
   Greg, 115.

15 *S.T.C.* 15028 —A pleasant conceited comedie, called, a knacke
      to knowe an honest man. 4°. *f. C. Burby,* 1596. Ent. 26 no.
      1595.
   Greg, 139, thinks the printer was either Thomas Scarlet or Robert
   Robinson.

16 Shakspere; *S.T.C.* 22294 —A pleasant conceited comedie called

Loues labors lost. Newly corrected and augmented by W. Shakespere. 4°. *W. W[hite] f. C. Burby,* 1598. Ent. to N. Ling with consent of Burby 22 ja. 1607.

Greg, 150.

17 Love's Labor Won. No edition known. Mentioned also by Meres, *Palladis Tamia,* 1598, who says it is Shakspere's.

18, 19, 20 This set of Ovid was in sixteens. The only complete set so far known to have been printed in this format in England was by Thomas Vautrollier in 1582-3 (*S.T.C.* 18927, 18928, and not in *S.T.C.;* see *Small Latine,* I, 512). The Vautrollier set is a re-print of the Plantin form, and Vautrollier also imported books from the Plantin press. The set of three listed in our manuscript was probably imported by some London dealer.

19b–20b Deloney; *S.T.C.* 6555 —The gentle craft. [Init. T. D.] 4°. *f. R. Bird,* 1637. Ent. to R. Blore, 19 oc. 1597; to E. Brewster a. R. Bird, 4 au. 1626.

6556 —The gentile craft. The second part. [Init. T. D.] 4°. *E. Purslow,* 1639. Ent. to R. Cotes, 9 no. 1633.

21 This would be some edition of the *Flores Senecæ* by Erasmus, col-lected from the prose. No edition is known to have been printed in England by this date.

21b Several early editions, the latest before the date of our manuscript being

S.T.C. 1990 —[Anr. ed.] Sir Bevis of Hampton. 4°. *T. East* [1582?]. Ent. 12 mr. 1582.

22 This would be *Sententiæ Ciceronis, Demosthenis, ac Terentii,* universally used in grammar-school work (*Small Latine,* Index). *S.T.C.* 5319 —Sententiæ Ciceronis. 12°. *T. Vautrollerius,* 1584.

5320 —Sententiæ Ciceronis, Demosthenis, ac Terentii. 8°. *ap. R. Dexter,* 1603.

The edition of 1603 is simply another edition, with the same title, of this long-established textbook.

22b Lupton; *S.T.C.* 16947 —A dream of the Deuill and Diues. 8°. *J. Charlwood f. H. Car,* 1584. Ent. 6 my. 1583.

16948 —[Anr. ed.] 8°. *E. Allde f. E. White,* 1615. Ent. 17 fb. 1603.

23 Ravisius, Joannes. *S.T.C.* 20763 —Epithetorum epitome. Accedunt Synonyma poetica. 16°. [*J. Jackson*] *pro* [*J. Harrison?* 1564?].

[Anr. ed.] *Ex off. Henrici Middletoni, pro Iohanne Harisono,* 1579. [U. of Ill. Lib.]

The reference may, however, be to some imported edition in full form or epitome.

23b Edwards; *S.T.C.* 7516 —The paradyse of dainty deuises. 4°. *H. Disle,* 1576. Ent. 3 de.

7517 —[Anr. ed.] The paradyse of daynty deuises. 4°. *H. Disle,* 1578.

7518 —[Anr. ed.] The paradyse of daintie deuises. 4°. *H. Dizle,* 1580.

7519 —[Anr. ed.] The paradise of daintie deuises. 4°. [n.p.] 1580. Ent. to T. Rider 26 jy. 1582.

7520 —[Anr. ed.] 4°. *R. Waldegraue f. E. White,* 1585. Ent. 11 ap. 1584.

7521 —[Anr. ed.] The paradice of dainty deuises. 4°. *E. Allde f. E. White,* 1596.

7522 —[Anr. ed.] 4°. *E. A*[*llde*] *f. E. White,* [1598?].

7523 —[Anr. ed.] 4°. *f. E. White,* 1600.

For a more detailed and more accurate account of editions, see the edition by Hyder E. Rollins.

24 *S.T.C.* 17286 —Manuzio, Paolo. Epistolarum libri x; eiusdem quæ præfationes appellantur, etc. 8°. *J. Kyngston f. W. Norton,* 1573. (*Excusum impensis Gulielmi Nortoni,* 1573. [U. of Ill. Lib.])

17287 —[Anr. ed.] Epistolarum libri x; quinque nuper additis. 16°. *T. Vautrollerius,* 1581.

17288 —[Anr. ed.] Epistolarum libri xii. 16°. *R. Robinsonus,* 1591.

17289 —[Anr. ed.] 16°. *R. Dexter,* 1603.

A most elegantly empty book, copies of which are much underscored for phrases; Manutius had himself compiled the universally used textbook of phrases.

[35]

24b Deloney; *S.T.C.* 6559 —The pleasant history of John Winchcomb, called Jack of Newberie. Now the eight time imprinted. [Init. T. D.] 4°. *H. Lownes, 1619.* Ent. to T. Millington, 7 mr. 1597, a. to H. Lownes, 25 my. 1597.

25 Augustine; *S.T.C.* 929 —The glasse of vaine-glorie. *Tr. W. P.*[rid]. 12°. *J. Windet, 1585.* Ent. 1 fb.
930 —[Anr. ed.] 12°. *J. Windet, 1587.*
931 —[Anr. ed.] 12°. *J. Windet, 1600.*

26–27 *S.T.C.* 9209 —Orders thought meete to be executed in places infected with the plague. [30 July 1603.] 4°. *R. Barker, 1603.*

28 Ruthven; *S.T.C.* 21466 —The Earl of Gowries conspiracie against the Kings maiestie of Scotland. 4°. *V. Simmes, 1600.* Ent. 11 se.
21467 —[Anr. ed.] 4°. *V. Simmes, 1603.*

29 Jewel; *S.T.C.* 14603 —An exposition upon the two Epistles to the Thessalonians. 8°. *R. Newberie a. H. Bynneman, 1583.* Ent. 24 fb.
14604 —[Anr. ed.] 8°. *R. Newberie, 1584.*
14605 —[Anr. ed.] 8°. *f. R. Newberie, 1594.*

30 Napier; *S.T.C.* 18354 —A plaine discouery of the whole Reuelation of Saint John. 4°. *Edinburgh, R. Waldegraue, 1593.*
18355 —[Anr. ed.] Newlie imprinted. 4°. [*Edinburgh, R. Waldegraue f.*] *J. Norton,* [*London,*] 1594.

31 King; *S.T.C.* 14976 —Lectures upon Jonas, 1594. 4°. *Oxford, J. Barnes, solde* [*by Joan Brome*], 1597. Ent.
14977 —[Anr. ed.] Newlie corrected. 4°. *solde* [*by Joan Brome*], *Oxford, J. Barnes,* 1599.
14978 —[Anr. ed.] 4°. *Oxford, J. Barnes, solde* [*by Joan Brome*], 1600. Ent. to P. Short a. T. Haies, 31 ja. 1602.

32 Babington; *S.T.C.* 1086 —Certaine plaine, briefe, and comfortable notes upon euerie chapter of Genesis. 4°. *f. T. Charde,* 1592. Ent. 8 no. 1591.
1087 —[Anr. ed.] Perused again and enlarged. 4°. *J. R*[oberts] *f. T. Charde,* 1596.

33 See line 28, above.

34 Dod; *S.T.C.* 6967 —A treatise or exposition vpon the ten com-
mandements. 8°. *f. T. Man,* 1603. Ent. 6 se. [Entry not found.]

34b *S.T.C.* 23886 —Comoediae sex, ex A. Mureti exemplari. 4°. *T.
Marsh,* 1583.
23887 —P. Terentii Afri comoediae sex. 12°. *Cantabrigiæ, ex
off. J. Legatt,* 1589.
23888 —[Anr. ed.] 12°. *ex off. R. Robinsoni,* 1597.
The Terence in our list is more likely to have been foreign printed.

35 Bilson; *S.T.C.* 3068 —A sermon preached before the King a.
Queenes majesties at their coronation. 8°. *V. S[ims] f. C.
Knight,* 1603. Ent. 9 au.

35b *S.T.C.* 5266 —M. T. Cic. De Officiis, de Senectute, de Amicitia,
Paradoxa, Somniũ Scipionis. 8°. *T. Vautrollerius,* 1579.
5267 —[Anr. ed.] *Ex typ. viduæ Orwin,* 1595.
I have: De Officiis M. T. Ciceronis Libri Tres. Item, De Amicitia:
De Senectute: Paradoxa: & de Somnio Scipionis. 8°. *ap. Ioan-
nem Kyngstonem,* 1574.
[Anr. ed.] 8°. *Ex Typographia Vidvæ Georgii Robinsoni,* 1587.
The University of Illinois has:
[Anr. ed.] 8°. *Ex Typographia Thomæ Orwinni,* 1590.
[Anr. ed.] 8°. *Ex Typographia Thomæ Orwinni,* 1593.
The edition of 1579 is of a different form from the others listed.
The four copies of our list are likely from some other English
printed edition nearer in date to 1603. The number of copies indi-
cates that this is not likely the translation.

36 Rudd; *S.T.C.* 21433 —A sermon preached before the kings maj-
estie at Greenwich. 8°. *J. H[arrison] f. T. Man a. C. Knight,*
1603. Ent. 27 jn.

37 Thorne; *S.T.C.* 24041 —Ἔσοπτρον βασιλικόν. Or, a kenning-
glasse for a christian king. 8°. *R. R[ead] f. J. Harrison,* 1603.
Ent. 15 jn.

38 Dove; *S.T.C.* 7084 —A perswasion to the English recusants, to
reconcile themselves to the Church of England. 4°. *V. S[ims]
f. C. Burby,* 1602.
7085 —[Anr. ed.] 4°. *V. S[ims] f. C. Burby,* 1603.

39   Muriell; *S.T.C.* 18292 —An answer unto the Catholiques supplica-
tion, etc. [Anon.] 4°. *R. R[ead] f. F. Burton,* 1603. Ent. 25 jn.

40   Indecipherable.

Second Leaf *Recto*

[1607, FRONT HINGE]

x Item a letter to Edward Digges to be
x delivered at ye Bishops house in pater noster
x row next ye kings hed in London September 1607
x abysed at c ... p c
x primers at m ... y c bo
x testaments at ... p 25
x ...

A playing cards   bodged for   yellow lattin
large gross horne ...horne   smal brass robnetes
middell Inkell   ...ringd   ... rings
crimson Inkell poz 8   best small howre glasses
A ff Inkell ... fillting   ... stones w'th sandes
... cotton Inkhornes   other ... stones w'th ould
rall ... ... pomades   knots   ... sparm ... sandes
... Inkhorne   of box   lattin bells
... Inkhornes w'th sandboxes balles
... white pins ... bookes   handglasses
... white pins ... green)   brushes

large white pins
Red & white pins y rose & prices   peni bed silk
peni flayed thred   topeny bred silk
topeny flayed thred   ... ation 2 3 4 6
robenty thred   bred silke & bells
large flat thred large ... Red   ... 2 3 4 bred
biol ... poynts   blak 2 3 4 bred silk
white paslbordes   plotted silk poynts
tenty pins no 6 7 8   girdles of sondry
box combes 1 grose   ... ... lases
Raw thred Inkell   looking glasses
peny thred ...
A narow white tape Inkell   ...
callinges   ...
middell tape w'th yellow far   yellow wax candles
... of grene Inkell
pees of narow yellow Inkell to string Inkhornes w'th

1	direct a letter to edward dighte to be		
2	delivered at christofer hvnts in pater noster		
3	rew'nere ye Kings hed in london september 1607		

1 direct a letter to edward dighte to be

2 delivered at christofer hvnts in pater noster

3 rew'nere ye Kings hed in london september 1607

4 absyes at C^s pr C

5 primers at m^s pr C

6 testaments at R^s pr 25

7	ff playing cards	lardgest pen	yellow lattin
8	lardg shewhornes	& Inkornes	smale bras covnters
9	middell Inkell	stringed	hog ringes
10	crimson Inkell pec[e]s		best smale hower glasses
11	ff ff Inkell & filleting		slekstones wth handels
12	hole bottom Inkhornes	knots	other slekstones w^thoute
13	calvs lether pennars	of box	spannish andels handels
14	vise Inkhornes	seales	lattin bels
15	vise Inkhornes wth sand boxes		
16	Red & white pins [ste]d boote		Hand flaskets
17	red & white pins [ ] boote & crovn[e]		brushes
18	lardg white pins		peni bred silk
19	Red & white pins ye rose & crovne		topeny bred silk
20	peni skayne thred		carnation 2^d/3^d/4^d–6^d bred silke silk
21	topeny skayne thred		grene 2^d/3^d/ & 4^d bred
22	coventry thred		blak 2^d/3^d/4^d bred silk
23	lardg flat thred laces & som Rovnd		plotted silk poynts
24	vilet lether poynts		girdels of sondry sortes
25	white past bords		
26	turkey pins no 6/7–8		tinsell & laste
27	box combs 1 grose		looking glases
28	Raw thred Inkell		
29	pecing thred/Re[d] grene/ purpel ashcullor/ blew/		
30	ff narow white tape Inkell		
31	Catlings		lynckes
32	mittins faced wth cullord fur		yelow wax candels
33	peces of grene Inkell		
34	peces of narow [c]ullord Inkell to string Inkhornes w^th		
35			

1   For Edward Dight, citizen, bookseller, and bookbinder of Exeter, see McKerrow, *Dictionary,* p. 92.

6   "R (in mediaeval notation) = 80" (*N.E.D.*)

7ff. Most of these items are self-explanatory or require only an ordinary dictionary. Where I have suspected the reader might have difficulty, I have attached a note. The exact archaeology of these items I must leave to the proper experts.

9   Inkle, "A kind of linen tape, formerly much used for various purposes" (*N.E.D.*). " 'What's the price of this inkle?' — 'One penny.' " (*Love's Labor's Lost,* III, 1, 139–40).

11b "Sleekstone. *Obs.* exc. *dial.* Also, 5 slek- . . . 1. A smooth stone used for smoothing and polishing . . . 1530 **Palsgr.** 720, I make paper smothe with a sleke stone . . . 1612 **Peacham** *Graphice* 94 Take of the fairest and smothest pastboord you can get, which with a sleeke stone rubbe as smooth, and euen as you can" (*N.E.D.*).

18 "Brede . . . sb.³, *arch.* Also . . . bred . . . [A variant of **Braid** *sb.,* in 16-17th c. . . .] 1. Anything plaited, entwined, or interwoven; a plait; interweaving, braiding, embroidery = **Braid,** *sb.* 4" (*N.E.D.*).

24b Plotted, platted.

27b Laste, evidently lace.

29 Pecing thred. "1594 *Acc.-Bk. W. Wray* in *Antiquary* XXXII. 347, 1 *li* pecinge thred, iis vj*d*" (*N.E.D.*).

35 This line contained prices on some item; but since I do not know what the item was, it would be pointless to attempt to decipher the remnants of the prices.

The text of this book, *Shakspere's "Love's Labor's Won,"* was composed and printed by The William Byrd Press, Inc., Richmond, Virginia, in an edition of 2,500 copies. The typeface is Baskerville, the display type is Bulmer. The collotypes were made by Meriden Gravure Company, Meriden, Connecticut. The book is printed on Curtis Colophon and bound by Russell Rutter Co., New York. It was designed by Willis A. Shell, Jr.